**W9-CAV-374**

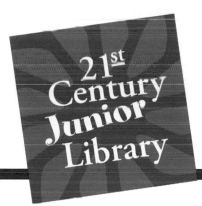

# NEPTUNE

by Ariel Kazunas

CHERRY LAKE PUBLISHING * ANN ARBOR, MICHIGAN

Published in the United States of America by Cherry Lake Publishing
Ann Arbor, Michigan
www.cherrylakepublishing.com

Content Adviser: Dr. Tobias Owen, University of Hawaii Institute for Astronomy

Photo Credits: Cover, ©Orlando Florin Rosu/Dreamstime.com; cover and pages 6, 12, 16, and 18, ©NASA; page 4, ©iStockphoto.com/alxpin; page 8, ©Byron W.Moore/Shutterstock, Inc.; page 10, ©iStockphoto.com/STEVECOLEccs; page 14, ©Science Photo Library/Alamy; page 20, ©ASSOCIATED PRESS

**LIBRARY OF CONGRESS CATALOGING-IN-PUBLICATION DATA**
Kazunas, Ariel.
  Neptune/by Ariel Kazunas.
    p. cm.—(21st century junior library)
  Includes bibliographical references and index.
  ISBN-13: 978-1-61080-083-9 (lib. bdg.)
  ISBN-10: 1-61080-083-4 (lib. bdg.)
  1. Neptune (Planet)—Juvenile literature. I. Title. II. Series.
  QB691.K39 2011
  523.48—dc22     2010052372

Cherry Lake Publishing would like to acknowledge the work of
The Partnership for 21st Century Skills.
Please visit www.21stcenturyskills.org for more information.

Printed in the United States of America
Corporate Graphics Inc.
July 2011
CLFA09

# CONTENTS

Neptune

Neptune is so far from Earth that we need a telescope to see it.

# Last in Line

**N**eptune is one of the eight planets in our **solar system**. It is almost four times bigger than Earth.

It is also the farthest planet from the Sun. We need **telescopes** to see it.

## Ask Questions!

We used to think our solar system had a ninth planet called Pluto. Pluto is very small. Scientists decided in 2006 that it was not a planet. Why? Ask your teacher or librarian to help you find out.

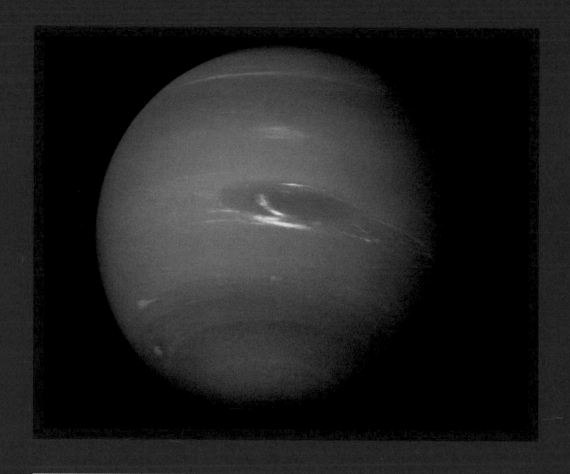

Neptune is known for its blue-green color.

It takes almost 165 Earth years for Neptune to **orbit** the Sun. This is because it is so far away from the Sun.

Neptune **rotates** very fast. The time it takes a planet to turn all the way around is one day. Earth's days are 24 hours long. Neptune's days are only 17 hours long!

Uranus gave scientists the clue they needed
to find Neptune.

# A Distant Discovery

**S**cientists once thought Uranus was the last planet in our solar system. Then they noticed that Uranus did not follow its orbit like it should. They decided that there must be another planet even farther away. That planet's **gravity** was causing Uranus' strange orbit.

A telescope is an important tool for anyone who wants to study our solar system.

The scientists used math to guess where the new planet might be. Then they looked at that spot through a telescope. Their idea was right! Neptune was just where they thought it would be.

**Make a Guess!**

You would need a very strong telescope to see Neptune in the sky. Why do you think this is? Remember how far away Neptune is.

*Voyager 2 was launched on August 20, 1977.*

# Rings and Moons

**A**bout 140 years went by before we learned much more about Neptune. NASA launched a spacecraft called *Voyager 2* in 1989. *Voyager 2* studied faraway planets. It sent back pictures showing rings around Neptune.

**Think!**

How do you think rings are formed? Only big planets have rings. Rings are mostly made of pieces of bigger objects that broke apart. Big planets have strong gravity. Could this help explain the rings?

There are six rings around Neptune.

Neptune's rings are very hard to see. There are billions of small pieces in each ring. Some of these pieces are slowly disappearing. Scientists think that one day all of the rings might disappear completely.

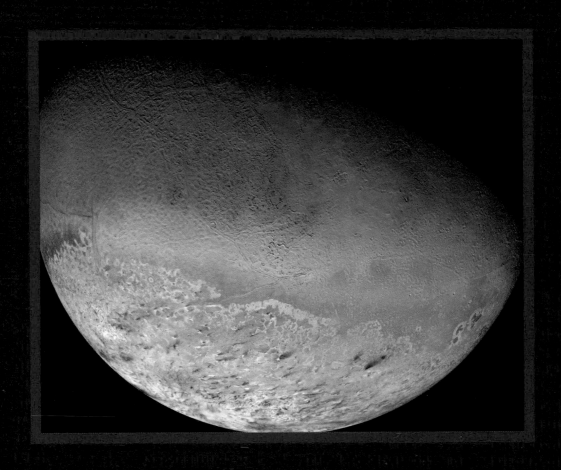

Triton is one of the largest moons in our solar system.

Scientists have found 13 moons orbiting Neptune. The biggest one is called Triton.

Scientists believe Triton formed somewhere else in the solar system. Neptune's strong gravity pulled Triton into its orbit. Triton orbits Neptune in the opposite direction of the rest of the moons.

The gas giants are the four largest planets in our solar system.

# A Gas Giant

Neptune is one of the planets known as gas giants. The others are Jupiter, Saturn, and Uranus. These planets are not solid. They are made mostly of gas.

Neptune is very cold. This is because it is so far from the Sun. The temperature at the top of Neptune's clouds is –353 degrees Fahrenheit (–214 degrees Celsius).

Neptune's storms show up as dark spots in photos.